HOW TO MANAGE
YOUR MONEY

WHEN YOU
DON'T HAVE ANY

Workbook

ERIK WECKS

ISBN: 978-1511734974

Table of Contents

HOW TO MANAGE
YOUR MONEY

WHEN YOU
DON'T HAVE ANY

Workbook

The Financial Master Plan

Your Financial Mission:

To secure your basic needs both now and in the future, and to do nothing that would harm your ability to secure them on an ongoing basis.

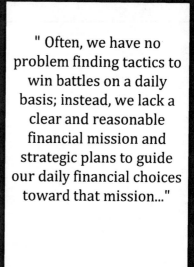

" Often, we have no problem finding tactics to win battles on a daily basis; instead, we lack a clear and reasonable financial mission and strategic plans to guide our daily financial choices toward that mission..."

Three Strategies to Accomplish Your Mission:

1. Live below your means and save the rest for a rainy day.

2. If at all possible, live without using debt.

3. Follow a financial road map.

A Financial Road Map That Supports Your Mission:

Step 0: On a monthly basis, make sure you are not spending more than you earn.

Step 1: Secure your basic needs: food, clothing, and shelter.

Step 2: Create a $1,000 emergency fund.

Step 3: Pay off all debts as fast as possible, other than your home.

Step 4: Increase your emergency fund until it reaches six to ten months of your basic needs.

Step 5: Begin saving 15 percent of your income for retirement.

Step 6: If so desired, save for your child's college education.

Step 7: Pay off your mortgage early.

Step 8: Express your values with your money.

Tactics That Bring Your Strategies to Life

Live by a zero-balance budget, created at least monthly.
Use cash whenever possible, to avoid busting your budget.

Introduction

So I've wanted to create a workbook for *How to Manage Your Money When You Don't Have Any* ever since I published the book. Then the book took off, and it felt like a simple, short workbook wasn't good enough. For a while I toyed with creating an app.

Now, three years later, I am finally getting around to writing a second edition of the book, and the time seems right to do what I wanted to do in the first place: to create a simple workbook that will allow readers to put into practice what they learned.

Just to be clear, this book is meant to supplement *How to Manage Your Money When You Don't Have Any*. There will be times where I refer to the book. To get maximum benefit from this workbook, take a little time and read that first. It will help make sense of the exercises here.

Feel free to make as many personal copies as you need of anything in the book. Just don't post them on-line or give them to your whole church. Writing is how I make my living, and I do my best to charge no more than fair price for my work.

Finally, a huge thank-you to the sixty thousand households who have been helped by *How to Manage Your Money When You Don't Have Any*. I'm really grateful to all of you, and I love hearing your stories. I hope the workbook helps you continue your journey toward financial stability.

Part 1:
Getting Ready to
Make Changes

Money and Me

The following section is designed to get you thinking about your current relationship to money. I'm a firm believer that lasting change takes a willingness to examine our current patterns of behavior and see why they don't match up with our desired values.

At the end of 2014, American consumers carried $860,000,000,000 in consumer debt.

What do you hope to get from this workbook?

_____

_____

_____

_____

_____

_____

_____

What circumstances have led you to want to find better financial stability?

_____

_____

_____

_____

_____

_____

When you think of the American dream, what do you think about?

_____

_____

_____

_____

_____

_____

"In America we have a better opportunity to be free from want than in just about any other place in the world....
Yet, from the earliest days of our nation, this modest American dream has always competed with a more grandiose version. This grand American dream might be stated as freedom to have *everything* I want."

Are you willing to give up on having "everything you want" in order to have less stress and more stability in your life? Why or why not?

_____

_____

_____

_____

List as many as ten of your fears about money and changing the way you handle it. Then go back and rank them from greatest (1) to least (10).

Fear
Rank

_____ ____

_____ ____

_____ ____

_____ ____

_____ ____

_____ ____

_____ ____

_____ ____

_____ ____

_____ ____

Addiction counselor Michael Dye argues that an implicit lose-lose double bind exists whenever our behavior doesn't match our desired values. Change requires a willingness to examine our double binds and to resolve them. To resolve them, we must be willing to do the hard thing we have been avoiding.

Take your list of ten fears, and write out the lose-lose double bind for the top five. Then write down the hard choice required for lasting change to take place. I've given an example below.

Fear 1:

I'm afraid to get rid of my credit cards because I believe that I won't be able live without the safety net they provide.

Lose/Lose Double bind: If I don't have any credit cards and there is an emergency, I won't have the money I need to protect my family. On the other hand, my family suffers because of the payments we have to make to the credit-card company every month.

The Hard Thing to Do: Save money for an emergency fund, which will might make my situation feel even worse for a while, and then live frugally until we pay off our debt.

Fear 1:

_____

_____

_____

Your Lose-Lose Double bind:

_____

_____

_____

_____

The Hard Thing to Do:

_____

_____

_____

_____

Fear 2:

_____

_____

_____

Your Lose-Lose Double bind:

_____

_____

_____

_____

The Hard Thing to Do:

_____

_____

_____

_____

Fear 3:

_____

_____

_____

Your Lose-Lose Double bind:

_____

_____

_____

_____

The Hard Thing to Do:

_____

_____

_____

_____

Fear 4:

_____

_____

_____

Your Lose-Lose Double bind:

_____

_____

_____

_____

The Hard Thing to Do:

_____

_____

_____

_____

Fear 5:

_____

_____

_____

Your Lose-Lose Double bind:

_____

_____

_____

_____

The Hard Thing to Do:

_____

_____

_____

_____

Fear 6:

_____

_____

_____

Your Lose-Lose Double bind:

_____

_____

_____

_____

The Hard Thing to Do:

_____

_____

_____

_____

Fear 7:

_____

_____

_____

Your Lose-Lose Double bind:

_____

_____

_____

_____

The Hard Thing to Do:

_____

_____

_____

_____

Fear 8:

_____

_____

_____

Your Lose-Lose Double bind:

_____

_____

_____

_____

The Hard Thing to Do:

_____

_____

_____

_____

Fear 9:

_____

_____

_____

Your Lose-Lose Double bind:

_____

_____

_____

_____

The Hard Thing to Do:

_____

_____

_____

_____

Fear 10:

_____

_____

_____

Your Lose-Lose Double bind:

_____

_____

_____

_____

The Hard Thing to Do:

_____

_____

_____

_____

Congratulations! You just conquered your first mountain on the way to better financial healthy. That's awesome!

Right about now, you may be feeling what author Brené Brown likes to call a vulnerability hangover. Your survival brain, that part of you that tries to keep you alive, is likely screaming that change is impossible, and you might as well give up. It has strong chemicals on its side, and its not afraid to use them in its war against the rational part of your brain.

It's important to remember that it takes two sides to have a war. Your rational brain doesn't have to fight the fear and anxiety produced by your survival brain. It can simply graciously accept it as an important part of you without letting it determine your actions. It's OK to be scared and still do the good thing.

I find it really helpful when anxious to remember that no matter what it feels like at this moment in time, there is no bear eating me. All that fear and anger is about a future that may or may not come to pass. Take a deep breath, and let it out slowly. Then remember that you already know that the path you are currently on won't work. That's why you bought this workbook.

If you want to make a change, you're going to have to do a little chemical warfare of your own. You're going to need to practice some strong self-compassion. We'll talk more about that in a later section. For now give yourself a pat on the back. You've done something that is quite difficult. You've faced your fears.

Your Money World

"The postwar dominance of taste and opinion in our culture's financial thinking created a whole host of new business opportunities. Luxury items and services designed to improve our quality of life took on a new importance.... Today consumer spending accounts for nearly 70 percent of our economic growth."

In this section, we'll look at how the world around us shapes our personal financial values and our view of money. Parents, neighbors, and the culture at large all have a say. To change, we will have to challenge these voices.

What do you remember about how your parents or caregivers handled money when you were a child? Were they good with money? Did they teach you money management skills? Did you grow up poor or well off?

_____

_____

_____

_____

_____

How does your upbringing affect your view of money today?

_____

_____

_____

_____

_____

What did they teach you about careers? Did their material wants cause them to have to work a job they hated, or were they more modest in their expectations in life? Which did they value more: time or their lifestyle?

_____

_____

_____

_____

_____

How do their choices affect how you view your career today? Does your work come from fear and worry, or do you find satisfaction and joy in your labor? Do you believe that hating your job is normal and expected? Do you sacrifice your time to keep a certain lifestyle?

_____

_____

_____

_____

_____

How do your friends and neighbors think about money? Do they value status-based consumption? Do they live beyond their means, using debt for cars and vacations? Are they poor with no hope of a better life?

_____

_____

_____

_____

_____

How do your relationships affect how you spend money? Do you feel the need to keep up with the Joneses? Do you fear becoming too big for your britches, too successful? Do you believe you are meant to stay poor?

_____

_____

_____

_____

_____

Are there financial secrets that you hide from family or friends? Is there anything embarrassing you wouldn't want others to know?

_____

_____

_____

_____

_____

_____

_____

_____

_____

Did this section bring up any new fears and double binds? If so, you can write them down here.

Fear:

_____

_____

_____

Lose-Lose Double bind:

_____

_____

_____

_____

The Hard Thing to Do:

_____

_____

_____

_____

Fear:

_____

_____

_____

Lose-Lose Double bind:

_____

_____

_____

_____

The Hard Thing to Do:

_____

_____

_____

_____

Compassionate Acceptance

This chapter offers a basic primer on self-acceptance. Don't get hung up here. If it isn't what you need, move on. The fact remains, true, lasting change starts when we accept our current situation without judgement.

Self-acceptance isn't self-help mubojumbo. It is a major component in third-wave behavioral therapies. Science based studies of the brain show strong benefits when we avoid judging ourselves.

More and more scientific studies demonstrate the value of self-acceptance. Suppressing our thoughts, our emotions, or our unwanted behaviors only makes them worse. Study after study shows that when we try to avoid an unwanted emotion or thought, we make it all the more likely that our mind will focus on just the thing we are trying to avoid.

If you want to know more about the science behind this, I suggest looking up the work of psychologist Stephen Hayes. His workbook *Get Out of Your Mind and Into Your Life* is a great tool for a close examination of these processes. If you have compulsive spending habits that you don't seem able to control, it might provide you with answers and an unexpected way forward.

In this section, I intend to cover only the basics of how to practice the principles of willing acceptance to untangle the double binds you examined in the previous section.

In *How to Manage Your Money When You Don't Have Any*, I argue that when you spend your money, you are expressing your values as you see them at that moment in time. It isn't someone else who decided that the payments on a new luxury car were more important than a proper emergency fund. It was you, and in that moment, you valued possessing a status car more than your security. Often, it isn't very long before we find ourselves regretting such choices.

So what happened here? Michael Dye would say that we had a disconnect between our expressed values and our aspired values. Such disconnects are behind all the double binds you wrote out in the first two sections of this book.

So what do you do about such internal double binds? How do you fix them? (What I say next may be a little counterintuitive. Hang with me, ok?) You don't. You learn to accept them. You learn even to compassionately embrace them as part of the human condition. Then, once you have settled in your mind that you don't have to act on what you feel, you take action based on your aspired values.

Compassionate acceptance of our unwanted thoughts and feelings is the only way forward. Remember what we said at the top of the page? There really isn't any hope if we try to resist our unwanted emotions or thoughts. We only end up making them worse. Self-acceptance of even those parts of us that make us uncomfortable is the only hope we have to find the room we need to make the choices we want.

The series of questions that follow are intended to help you walk through the double binds we saw in the earlier sections of this workbook and so find the freedom we need to make our actions match up with our aspired values.

"Acceptance is the first step toward change. When I reserve judgment on my actions, I am often much more able to understand what motivates my behavior, and this lets me move forward.... Once we stop, we can relax and find a way out of our dilemma.."

Lose-Lose Double bind:

_____

_____

Examine each side of the double bind separately. What do you observe about each? What emotions do they bring? What beliefs and thoughts do they bring? (Avoid embracing or resisting these uncomfortable feelings and thoughts. Just observe them.)

_____

_____

_____

_____

When you think about "the hard thing to do," what emotions follow? Are you willing to have compassion toward these?

_____

_____

_____

_____

List any tools, skills, or people who can help you take action to do the hard thing.

_____

_____

_____

_____

What three steps are you willing to take to start resolving your double bind this week?

1._____

_____

2._____

_____

3._____

_____

(Make copies of this page for each of your double binds. If that is too much, consider working on one a week until you have resolved all of them.)

Anger primarily functions to numb pain and give us the energy needed to fight off a hungry grizzly bear. That's why it's so useful when we get afraid. We feel brave and empowered.

However, when used to numb our anxiety, it's a short-term fix. The fear returns, often with shame. Compassion is sustainable. Anger isn't.

A 2013 study in the *Journal of Clinical Psychology* (vol. 1) found that participants in an eight-week self-compassion course had better well-being than a control group six months and a year later.

Part 2: Forward-Looking Budgets

Expenses

According to the Bureau of Labor and Statistics, in 2013 an average American household of four spent about $7925 on food, $3120 of which was spent on eating away from home.

"When I say the word budget, many people think all I mean are their monthly bills. They imagine the rest of their money as a big pile from which everything else is taken as needed. They often have no idea how much is spent on food, gasoline, eating out or coffee. "

The first step in creating a practical, workable budget that accounts for everything you spend in a month comes from... wait for it... knowing what you spent last month. So yes, a forward-looking budget starts with looking backward. This exercise will take some time, so be prepared to put in a little effort here.

On the next page, you will find a list of suggested monthly expense categories. This list is by no means comprehensive, and you might find a different list much more helpful for you. Better still, make your own categories that reflect your way of thinking about money. If you find them unhelpful, you can always change them later.

Now comes the difficult part. Either on a piece of scratch paper, or better yet on a spreadsheet, categorize all the money your household spent last month. This includes money spent by debit card, credit card, cash, Paypal, online subscription, or any other means of payment. It would be hard to overemphasize how much it will help you in the future to be comprehensive here. Those little purchases online or on your phone need to be counted as well.

That said, it isn't as important to be exact as it is to be comprehensive. I don't think it will hurt to round things to the nearest dollar or estimate what that coffee date or lunch cost. The goal is to end up with a working knowledge of how much you spent on items like food, transportation, and entertainment.

To help you as you work through your budgeting process, I have included budgets for four different households. They are designed to give you an insiders look at how other families use this budgeting process to improve their financial stability. If you get stuck at any point don't hesitate to jump ahead and look at their work.

Be careful you don't hide important information from yourself when you categorize your expenses. For instance, it wouldn't do any good to use a euphemism like "online purchases" to cover up an out-of-control mobile app habit. Clarity and honesty matter when you categorize your spending.

Giving

College Fund

Groceries

School Lunches

Emergency Fund

Necessary Clothing

Mortgage

Gasoline

Bus Pass

Car Repairs/Maintenance

Home Repairs

Electricity

Retirement Fund

Water

Vacation Fund

Internet Access

Rent

Phones

Trash

Medical Bills

Cable

Natural Gas

Furniture/Appliances

Medical Insurance

Prescriptions

Home Owners/Renters Insurance

Auto Licensing

HOA Fees

Haircuts

Dry Cleaning

Dentist

Auto Insurance

Household Products

Parking Fees

Cosmetics

Glasses/Contacts

Date Night

Necessary Personal Products

Gym Membership

Eating Out

Chore Money for Kids

Entertainment

Software

Netflix/Spotify/iTunes

Video Games

Credit Cards

Student Loans

Car Payment

Other Debts

Fashion

Category	No. of Transactions	Total for the Month
_____	_____	$_____
_____	_____	$_____
_____	_____	$_____
_____	_____	$_____
_____	_____	$_____
_____	_____	$_____
_____	_____	$_____
_____	_____	$_____
_____	_____	$_____
_____	_____	$_____
_____	_____	$_____
_____	_____	$_____
_____	_____	$_____
_____	_____	$_____
_____	_____	$_____
_____	_____	$_____
_____	_____	$_____
_____	_____	$_____
_____	_____	$_____
_____	_____	$_____
_____	_____	$_____
_____	_____	$_____
_____	_____	$_____
_____	_____	$_____
_____	_____	$_____
_____	_____	$_____
_____	_____	$_____
_____	_____	$_____
_____	_____	$_____
_____	_____	$_____
_____	_____	$_____

Total Amount Spent During the Month: $_____

_____ _____ $_____

_____ _____ $_____

_____ _____ $_____

_____ _____ $_____

_____ _____ $_____

_____ _____ $_____

_____ _____ $_____

_____ _____ $_____

_____ _____ $_____

_____ _____ $_____

_____ _____ $_____

_____ _____ $_____

_____ _____ $_____

_____ _____ $_____

_____ _____ $_____

_____ _____ $_____

_____ _____ $_____

_____ _____ $_____

_____ _____ $_____

_____ _____ $_____

_____ _____ $_____

_____ _____ $_____

_____ _____ $_____

_____ _____ $_____

_____ _____ $_____

_____ _____ $_____

_____ _____ $_____

_____ _____ $_____

Subtotal from This Page: $_____

Subtotal from Previous Page: **+** $_____

Total Amount Spent During the Month: **=** $_____

"Step 0" Check

OK, surprise inspection here. Now that you have your expenses for the month, it's time to make sure you didn't spend more than you brought home last month. First things first. Calculate your take home pay. This is the amount of cash you have available to meet your needs each month. Once that is done, subtract the amount you spent last month from your income. Hopefully you end up with a positive number. If not, you will need to make some serious cuts when we get to making a budget in the next section.

Income Source   Total for the Month

_____ $_____

_____ $_____

_____ $_____

_____ $_____

_____ $_____

_____ $_____

_____ $_____

_____ $_____

                 Total Income: $_____

             Total Expenses: - $_____

Remaining Income/Monthly Shortfall: = $_____

So is your boat floating or sinking? If you have a large sum left over, double-check to make sure you cataloged your expenses accurately. If you did, congrats! It's time to get moving forward on those steps talked about in the master plan at the beginning of the book. If your number is negative, don't worry. That is often the case when a household first takes the step zero test. It means that you will have some work to do when we get to creating a budget.

Four Sample Households

According to FINRA.org, a 2013 survey found that households without emergency savings were three times more likely to make a late payment on their mortgage.

Looking forward always starts with looking backward. Samantha Smyle and Sarah and Tim Chan already know what they spend on a monthly basis. They are adjusting to new (or temporary) circumstances which alter their typical pattern. The other two households are just starting to get a grip on their financial reality.

Samantha Smyle

Sam Smyle was introduced in *How to Manage Your Money When You Don't Have Any*. You may remember her as Dr. Bite's front desk assistant. She has been divorced for a few years and since the divorce has already made strides to move her finances in the right direction. She is a few months away from completing a degree as a dental assistant. Sam already lives on a zero-balance budget. Now however, she's facing a real crisis. Due to an economic downturn her already tight budget is getting tighter. Dr. Bite has cut her hours and asked her to contribute to her health insurance. What she spent last month won't work this month. She will have to find a way to make things work.

Category	No. of Transactions	Total for the Month
Rent	1	$ 850.00
Groceries	7	$ 500.00
Personal and Household	4	$ 75.00
Gasoline	5	$ 65.00
Renters and Auto Insurance	1	$ 110.00
Electricity	1	$ 85.00
Emergency Savings	1	$ 45.00
Cable TV / Internet	1	$ 80.00
Cell Phones	1	$ 100.00
College Tuition	1	$ 50.00
Entertainment and Eating Out	2	$ 50.00
Pocket Money	5	$ 100.00
Savings for a New Car	1	$ 200.00

Total Amount Spent During the Month: $ 2,3100.00

Bill and Betsy Bite

Dr. Bite was also introduced in the book. He is an upper middle class dentist who owns his own practice. Because of the recent financial crisis, Dr. Bite's income has taken a dramatic tumble over the last two years. Before the financial crisis, Bill and Betsy lived right at the edge of their income without any margin for a rainy day. Finally ready to face their situation, Bill and Betsy are going to have to make some tough choices to balance the budget. They place a high value on their children's education. They are willing to make some hard choices to preserve it.

Category	No. of Transactions	Total for the Month
First Mortgage	1	$2,800.00
Second Mortgage	1	$600.00
Groceries, etc.	9	$1,000.00
Household Products	3	$150.00
Personal Care Products	5	$100.00
Hair/Nails/Cosmetics	6	$200.00
Car Insurance	1	$220.00
Gasoline	11	$450.00
Electricity	1	$120.00
Natural Gas	1	$120.00
Water / Sewer	1	$85.00
Garbage	1	$85.00
Cable TV / Internet	1	$220.00
Cell Phones	1	$150.00
Student Loan	1	$967.00
Minimum Credit Card Payments	4	$612.00
Car Payment	1	$425.00
Private School Payments	1	$1,500.00
Entertainment and Eating Out	6	$300.00
Pocket Money	13	$250.00
Vacation Fund	1	$100.00

Total Amount Spent During the Month: $10,454.00

Janelle Williams and Marco Brown

College graduates in their late mid twenties, Janelle and Marco moved in together a few months ago. Finances have been a topic of hot conversation. From the beginning, Marco wanted to combine their finances and work together to share the load. He felt it was a generous offer, considering he has the larger salary. However, Janelle's parents never communicated about money except when they fought. They also struggled to make ends meet much more than Marco's parents. She's always been careful not to repeat their mistakes. She was nervous about combining her money with Marco, but in the end she reluctantly agreed. Now Janelle is more than a little frustrated with some of Marco's spending habits. They are making ends meet, but they have little set aside for a rainy day. When Marco's car broke down and they used the credit card for food, he finally agreed that something has to change.

Category	No. of Transactions	Total for the Month
Rent	1	$ 750.00
Groceries	3	$ 400.00
Household/Personal Products	2	$ 100.00
Electricity	1	$ 57.00
Cell Phone	1	$ 150.00
Internet	1	$ 88.00
Gasoline	4	$ 110.00
Bus Pass	1	$ 45.00
Insurance (Auto and Renters)	1	$ 140.00
Student Loans	1	$ 384.00
Car Payment	1	$ 250.00
Credit Card Minimum Payment	1	$ 143.00
Eating Out	7	$ 247.00
Concert Tickets	1	$ 220.00
Board Games/Video Games/Apps	11	$ 225.00

Total Amount Spent During the Month: $ 3,309.00

Sarah and Tim Chan

Sarah Chan and Tim Chan have always broken the mold. Sarah is a programmer for a large software company. Tim is a sculptor with a part-time graphic design gig on the side. He stays at home to raise their two school age kids. From the beginning, they were committed to living within their means and putting aside something for a rainy day. Now ten years into their marriage, they have a fully funded emergency fund of eight months of expenses. They save for retirement, and they pay extra on their mortgage. This month is back to school month. The kids need a few new things, *and* Sarah's younger sister is getting married. Last month's budget comes up short. They need to make temporary changes.

Category	No. of Transactions	Total for the Month
Giving	1	$ 600.00
Mortgage (1 1/2 Payments)	1	$ 1800.00
Groceries	6	$ 700.00
Household Products	4	$ 100.00
Personal Products/Haircuts	2	$ 150.00
Electricity	1	$ 130.00
Natural Gas	1	$ 87.00
Sewer/Water	1	$ 52.00
Garbage/Recycling	1	$ 64.00
Cell Phone	1	$ 145.00
Internet/HBO	1	$ 102.00
Gasoline	1	$ 300.00
Car Insurance	1	$ 145.00
Emergency Savings (Fully Funded)	0	$ 00.00
Next Car	1	$ 200.00
Vacation Fund	1	$ 200.00
School Supplies / Clothes	5	$ 200.00
Wedding/Shower Gifts	3	$ 150.00
Eating Out	3	$ 200.00
Boat Maintenance/Slip/Fuel	3	$ 258.00
Pocket Money	12	$ 120.00

Total Amount Spent During the Month: $ 5703.00

Samantha Smyle

Income Source	Total for the Month
Take-home Pay	$ **2057.37**
	$
Total Income:	$ **2057.37**
Total Expenses: -	$ **2310.00**
Remaining Income/Monthly Shortfall: =	$ **-252.63**

Bill and Betsy Bite

Income Source	Total for the Month
Dental Take-home Pay	$ **6,535.68**
	$
Total Income:	$ **6,535.68**
Total Expenses: -	$ **10,454.00**
Remaining Income/Monthly Shortfall: =	$ **-3,918.32**

Janelle Williams and Marco Brown

Income Source	Total for the Month
Marco's Take Home	$ 1,683.10
Janelle's Take Home	$ 1,575.71
Total Income:	$ 3,258.81
Total Expenses: -	$ 3,309.00
Remaining Income/Monthly Shortfall: =	$ -50.19

Sarah and Tim Chan

Income Source	Total for the Month
Sarah's Take Home	$ 4,013.57
Tim's Design Take Home	$ 1,286.62
Total Income:	$ 5,300.19
Total Expenses: -	$ 5,703.00
Remaining Income/Monthly Shortfall: =	$ -402.81

Budget

If you live in a household where you and your partner combine incomes, it's time to work separately. Each of you prepare your own zero-balance budget reflecting your values. Then come together to make your master budget.

"It's time to take back a sense of ownership over your money. Your money isn't forcing you to do anything. You get to make all the choices when it comes to your money. How you spend your money is simply an expression of your values. So express yourself. Just be honest about what you value, and be willing to take responsibility for your choices."

The zero-balance budget is the heart and soul of the changes I want to bring to your financial stability. A zero-balance budget allows you to look forward, anticipating next month's expenses, and then allocate funds based upon those expenses. When you master zero-balance budgeting, it will alter your financial thinking. When combined with an effective means for controlling your expenses, it will provide you with a clear and useable picture to assist you in directing your money where you want it to go.

On the next page, you will find a blank expense sheet like the one you used in the last section to categorize your expenses, and that is exactly what you will do again. Except in this case, you will categorize the expenses you anticipate next month and the amount you anticipate them to cost. I took the liberty of putting in a couple of suggested categories that I argue should be at the top of your list. Don't forget! An emergency fund is probably the most important item on the budget once you've paid for your food, clothing, shelter, and everything you need to support them for the next month.

When deciding how much to spend for a given item, the expense list you created can be your guide. Once you are done, make sure to leave several lines at the the bottom available for expenses that you forgot. This will happen, especially the first few times you use this budget.

Once you have all your expenses added to the budget, make sure you fund the "grease" category, or as I like to call it, the "humility" category. Humility or Grease acts as the contingency you leave in your budget for those things you forget. Especially when you first start, it should be a rather significant sum, something that could cover a missed light bill or the like.

The Humility category is important because a zero -based budget is designed to allocate every dollar of your take-home pay, so leaving some contingency for mistakes is essential.

Once you have an estimate of next month's expenses, you move on to do next month's "step 0" check. Just like the last section, you will add up all your sources of anticipated take-home pay for next month. Once you have your total take home pay, you will subtract your expenses. You will notice that the answer to that bit of math is pre-printed on the budget form. It will always equal "$0.00." In this way, the amount of money that you brought in for the month is exactly the amount of money you spent.

What should you do if your budget didn't equal the total amount of income you brought in for the month? You go back and trim or adjust categories until they match. Hopefully, you had extra money to put in savings. More likely, you needed to cut your expenses to match your income.

After you finish adjusting the budget, most of you will need to make one more step. In many households, the money for next month's cable bill isn't available right at the beginning of the month. That's OK. You will need to fill out the cash flow worksheet on the fourth page of the budget. This worksheet will help you make sure that all the bills get paid over the course of the next month without overdrawing your bank account. As you gain control of your finances, work to save until you can pay all of this month's needs with last month's money.

According to the 2014 NFCC Consumer Financial Literacy Survey, only 39% of American Adults said they used a budget of any sort.

Zero-Balance Budget Sheet

Cash Y/N	Pay Period No.	Category	Total for the Month
N	___	<u>Rent / Mortgage</u>	$_____
Y	___	<u>Groceries</u>	$_____
___	___	_____	$_____
___	___	_____	$_____
___	___	_____	$_____
___	___	_____	$_____
___	___	_____	$_____
___	___	_____	$_____
___	___	_____	$_____
___	___	_____	$_____
___	___	_____	$_____
___	___	_____	$_____
___	___	_____	$_____
___	___	_____	$_____
___	___	_____	$_____
___	___	_____	$_____
___	___	_____	$_____
___	___	_____	$_____
___	___	_____	$_____
___	___	_____	$_____
___	___	_____	$_____
___	___	_____	$_____
___	___	_____	$_____
		Subtotal:	$_____

—	—	———————————	$_____
—	—	———————————	$_____
—	—	———————————	$_____
—	—	———————————	$_____
—	—	———————————	$_____
—	—	———————————	$_____
—	—	———————————	$_____
—	—	———————————	$_____
—	—	———————————	$_____
—	—	———————————	$_____
—	—	———————————	$_____
—	—	———————————	$_____
—	—	———————————	$_____
—	—	———————————	$_____
—	—	———————————	$_____
—	—	———————————	$_____
—	—	———————————	$_____
—	—	———————————	$_____
—	—	———————————	$_____
—	—	———————————	$_____
—	—	———————————	$_____
—	—	———————————	$_____
—	—	———————————	$_____
—	—	———————————	$_____
—	—	———————————	$_____
—	—	———————————	$_____
—	—	———————————	$_____

Subtotal from this Page: $_____

Subtotal from Previous Page: **+** $_____

Total Amount to Spend During the Month: **=** $_____

Anticipated Income Source   Total for the Month

_____ $_____
_____ $_____
_____ $_____
_____ $_____
_____ $_____
_____ $_____
_____ $_____
_____ $_____
_____ $_____
_____ $_____

                    Total Income: $_____

                  Total Expenses: - $_____

                                              $_____
                                                  0.00

Items to Be Paid with Cash

_____ $_____
_____ $_____
_____ $_____
_____ $_____
_____ $_____
_____ $_____
_____ $_____
_____ $_____
_____ $_____
_____ $_____

              Total Cash Needed $_____

If you need to spend anticipated income to make your budget work, then you will need to fill out the Cash Flow Worksheet to make sure you only spend money after it arrives in your account.

Using the Income Worksheet on the facing page, figure out how much money will arrive each week and place each week in the Take Home column. Next, decide which items from your budget will be paid during each pay period and add them together to make sure you don't spend more than you brought in during the pay period. The week's total goes in the "Amount Spent" column. The remainder for the week becomes the Carry-Over for the next week. Finally, make sure you mark off these items on the budget, designating when they will be paid during the month. Some families find that the bills are paid on the first of each month, and the cash budget for groceries, etc., starts on the fifteenth of each month. There are many, many ways to manage your cashflow. As you practice, you will find a way that works for you.

Make sure that your "carry-over" number is always positive, or you will run out of money in your bank account and get charged for an overdraft!

Cash Flow Worksheet

No.	Date Executed	Carry Over (Last Pay Period Or Previous Month)	Take-Home Pay	Available Funds	Amount Spent	Carry-Over (Next Pay Period)
1	1-3-20xx	$0.00 +	$1236.35 =	$1236.35 -	$1192.86 =	$43.49
		$ +	$ =	$ -	$ =	$
		$ +	$ =	$ -	$ =	$
		$ +	$ =	$ -	$ =	$
		$	$	$	$	$

43

Sam Smyle's Zero-Balance Budget Sheet

Cash Y/N	Pay Period No.	Category	Total for the Month
___	___	Rent	$ 850.00
y	___	Groceries	$ 500.00
y	___	Personal and Household	$ 75.00
y	___	Gasoline	$ 65.00
___	___	Renters and Auto Insurance	$ 110.00
___	___	Electricity	$ 85.00
___	___	Emergency Savings	$ 50.00
___	___	Cable TV / Internet	$ 45.00
___	___	Cell Phones	$ 80.00
___	___	College Tuition	$ 100.00
___	___	Entertainment and Eating Out	$ 00.00
y	___	Pocket Money	$ 25.00
___	___	Savings for a New Car	$ 00.00
y	___	Soccer Fees	$ 50.00
___	___	Humility	$ 22.37

Income:			$ 2057.37
Expenses:	-		$ 2057.37
	=		$ 00.00

Cash Flow Worksheet

No.	Date Executed	Carry Over (Last Pay Period Or Previous Month)	Take Home	Available Funds	Amount Spent	Carry Over (Next Pay Period)
|	___	$ ___ +	$ ___ =	$ ___ -	$ ___ =	$ ___
|	___	$ ___ +	$ ___ =	$ ___ -	$ ___ =	$ ___
|	___	$ ___ +	$ ___ =	$ ___ -	$ ___ =	$ ___
|	___	$ ___	$ ___ =	$ ___ -	$ ___ =	$ ___
|	___	$ ___	$ ___ =	$ ___ -	$ ___ =	$ ___

Items to Be Paid with Cash

Groceries	$ 500.00
Personal and Household	$ 75.00
Gasoline	$ 65.00
Pocket Money	$ 25.00
Soccer Fees	$ 50.00
___	$ ___
___	$ ___
___	$ ___
___	$ ___
Total Cash Needed	$ 715.00

> Sam has balanced her budget in the only way she could. She has removed eating out and entertainment. When that wasn't enough she has reduced her monthly savings, eliminating setting aside any money for a new car. This isn't a huge problem because she drives little and already has several thousand dollars set aside. If she needed to, she could purchase a serviceable used vehicle for cash to replace her current car.

Bill and Betsy Bite's Zero-Balance Budget Sheet

Cash Y/N	Pay Period No.	Category	Total for the Month
___	___	Rent	$ 1,300.00
___	___	Second Mortgage	$ 00.00
Y	___	Groceries, etc.	$ 700.00
Y	___	Household Products	$ 75.00
Y	___	Personal Care Products	$ 75.00
Y	___	Haircuts	$ 25.00
___	___	Car Insurance	$ 220.00
Y	___	Gasoline	$ 350.00
___	___	Electricity	$ 160.00
___	___	Natural Gas	$ 45.00
___	___	Water / Sewer	$ 85.00
___	___	Garbage	$ 85.00
___	___	Cable TV / Internet	$ 120.00
___	___	Cell Phones	$ 150.00
___	___	Student Loan	$ 967.00
___	___	Minimum Credit Card Payments	$ 00.00
___	___	Car Payment	$ 425.00
___	___	Private School Payments	$ 1,500.00
___	___	Entertainment and Eating Out	$ 00.00
Y	___	Pocket Money	$ 50.00
Y	___	Daughter's Birthday	$ 75.00
___	___	Vacation Fund	$ 00.00
___	___	Emergency Savings	$ 100.00
___	___	Humility	$ 28.68
		Income:	$ 6535.68
		Expenses:	- $ 6535.68
			= $ 00.00

Cash Flow Worksheet

No.	Date Executed	Carry Over (Last Pay Period Or Previous Month)	Take Home	Available Funds	Amount Spent	Carry Over (Next Pay Period)
—	——	$____ +	$____ =	$____ -	$____ =	$____
—	——	$____ +	$____ =	$____ -	$____ =	$____
—	——	$____ +	$____ =	$____ -	$____ =	$____
—	——	$____	$____ =	$____ -	$____ =	$____
—	——	$____	$____ =	$____ -	$____ =	$____

Items to Be Paid with Cash

Groceries, etc.	$ *700.00*
Household Products	$ *75.00*
Personal Care Products	$ *75.00*
Haircuts	$ *25.00*
Gasoline	$ *75.00*
Pocket Money	$ *350.00*
Daughter's Birthday	$ *50.00*
	$ *75.00*
_____	$ _____
_____	$ _____
_____	$ _____
Total Cash Needed	$ *1350.00*

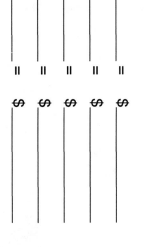

Facing up to financial reality has meant a bankruptcy for the Bite's. They also gave their home back to the bank. They eliminated both mortgages and their credit card payments. (Student loans are not available for bankruptcy, and they excluded their vehicle.) While the bankruptcy has made their situation tolerable, they still have had major lifestyle changes. However, they continue to pay for private school. Because of this choice, they remain incredibly fragile. If they faced a major emergency right now, they would be in real trouble because they have no emergency fund. Like Sam, they also receive only one paycheck per month.

Janelle Williams and Marco Brown's Zero-Balance Budget Sheet

Cash Y/N	Pay Period No.	Category	Total for the Month
—	1	Rent	$ 750.00
Y	2	Groceries	$ 400.00
Y	2	Household/Personal Products	$ 100.00
—	1	Electricity	$ 57.00
—	1	Cell Phone	$ 150.00
—	1	Internet	$ 88.00
Y	2	Gasoline	$ 110.00
Y	1	Bus Pass	$ 45.00
—	1	Insurance (Auto and Renters)	$ 140.00
—	1	Emergency Fund	$ 200.00
—	2	Student Loans	$ 384.00
—	2	Car Payment	$ 250.00
—	2	Credit Card Minimum Payment	$ 143.00
Y	2	Eating Out	$ 100.00
—	2	Concert Tickets	$ 00.00
Y	2	Board Games/Video Games/Apps	$ 150.00
Y	1	Pocket Money ($60/$60)	$ 120.00
—	—	Humility	$ 45.57

Income: $ 3,258.81

Expenses: - $ 3,258.81

= $ 00.00

Cash Flow Worksheet

No.	Date Executed	Carry Over (Last Pay Period Or Previous Month)		Take Home		Available Funds		Amount Spent		Carry Over (Next Pay Period)
		$	+	$	=	$	-	$	=	$
		$	+	$	=	$	-	$	=	$
1	2-1-20xx	$00.00	+	$1,629.40	=	$1,629.00	-	$1,550.00	=	$79.00
2	2-15-20xx	$79.00	+	$1,629.40	=	$1708.40	-	Remainder	=	$00.00

Items to Be Paid with Cash

Groceries	$400.00
Household/Personal Products	$100.00
Gasoline	$110.00
Bus Pass	$45.00
Eating Out	$100.00
Board Games/Video Games/Apps	$150.00
Pocket Money ($60/$60)	$120.00
	$
	$
	$
Total Cash Needed	**$1025.00**

Janelle and Marco have reprioritized their spending to make sure that they have enough for an emergency in the future. They are working on Step One of the financial plan, developing at least a $1,000 emergency fund. Once they have that money in the bank, they will shift their focus to paying off their debt. Using cash for online purchases can be difficult. Janelle and Marco set cash aside and then remove it from their their wallet when it is spent. That cash is stored in an envelope and brought back into the budget next month. In that way they limit themselves to their budgeted amount when making online purchases.

Sarah and Tim Chan's
Zero-Balance Budget Sheet

Cash Y/N	Pay Period No.	Category	Total for the Month
—	—	Giving	$600.00
—	—	Mortgage (1 1/2 Payments)	$1800.00
Y	—	Groceries	$700.00
Y	—	Household Products	$50.00
Y	—	Personal Products/Haircuts	$50.00
—	—	Electricity	$130.00
—	—	Natural Gas	$87.00
—	—	Sewer/Water	$52.00
—	—	Garbage/Recycling	$64.00
—	—	Cell Phone	$145.00
—	—	Internet/HBO	$102.00
Y	—	Gasoline	$300.00
—	—	Car Insurance	$145.00
—	—	Emergency Savings (FullyFunded)	$00.00
—	—	Next Car	$200.00
—	—	Vacation Fund	$00.00
Y	—	School Supplies / Clothes	$200.00
Y	—	Wedding/Shower Gifts	$150.00
Y	—	Eating Out	$50.00
—	—	Boat Maintenance/Slip/Fuel	$258.00
Y	—	Pocket Money	$120.00
—	—	Humility	$97.19

Income:	$5300.19
Expenses:	- $5300.19
	= $00.00

Cash Flow Worksheet

No.	Date Executed	Carry Over (Last Pay Period Or Previous Month)	Take Home	Available Funds	Amount Spent	Carry Over (Next Pay Period)
—		$ ___ +	$ ___ =	$ ___ -	$ ___ =	$ ___
—		$ ___ +	$ ___ =	$ ___ -	$ ___ =	$ ___
—		$ ___ +	$ ___ =	$ ___ -	$ ___ =	$ ___
—		$ ___	$ ___ =	$ ___ -	$ ___ =	$ ___
—		$ ___	$ ___ =	$ ___ -	$ ___ =	$ ___

Items to Be Paid with Cash

Groceries	$ 700.00
Household Products	$ 100.00
Personal Products / Haircuts	$ 150.00
Gasoline	$ 300.00
School Supplies / Clothes	$ 200.00
Wedding/Shower Gifts	$ 150.00
Eating Out	$ 200.00
Pocket Money	$ 120.00
	$ ___
	$ ___
Total Cash Needed	$ 1,920.00

Sarah and Tim have reduced their extraneous spending this month in order to pay for back-to-school clothing and supplies along with Sarah's sister's wedding gifts. Having a fully funded emergency fund and no debts other than their house, they were able to find the funds they needed by simply reducing their discretionary spending. Next month much of that spending will be restored. Don't be disheartened. This example isn't here to make you feel badly about your income. I included it to show the difference it can make when you live this way consistently for a long time. That will be true whatever your income level.

Conclusion

Getting the hang of zero-balance budgeting isn't rocket science, but if this is your first time using a zero-balance budget, don't expect to get it right in the first month. Usually in a week or three, you end up needing to have what my wife and I call an EBCM, an Emergency Budget Committee Meeting. In most cases, the emergency is solved by rejiggering our cash budget. Forgot school pictures this month? Then take a little from my pocket money, a little from our date, and even a little from the gas fund, and the problem is fixed. For the first few months, this kind of renegotiation is the norm.

For those of you scraping along the bottom right now, the last week of the month can be a real stretch. It's when we reach for the jar of peaches and make due with spaghetti for dinner. No one goes hungry, but we aren't eating steak, either.

Once you realize how calm your life can be without the terror and dread of debt and financial emergencies, such stretching becomes a joy, rather than a burden.

I hope you have found this workbook helpful. I depend upon my sales at Amazon to make my living. If you have found it useful, would you mind leaving me a review there? It would be a great help. Thanks, and good luck!

CPSIA information can be obtained
at www.ICGtesting.com
Printed in the USA
LVOW09s1048120617

537813LV00011B/218/P